Adventures of Penny and Molly

Copyright © 1990, 2022 by Ruth Carleton.

All rights reserved. No part of this book may be reproduced in any form without permission in writing from the author, except by reviewer who wishes to quote brief passages in connection with a review.

Acknowledgments

I would like to express my profound gratitude and appreciation to my dear friend Beatrice Duran for her unselfish efforts in assisting in sending the handwritten manuscript for layout and typesetting. Beatrice Duran also checked for accuracy of the typeset book.

I am also grateful to Gilford Denis for laying out and typesetting the book, and to Terry Denis for helping upload the book to Amazon. Thank you so much to both of you for helping make my published book a reality!

Finally, thank you to my daughter, Nancy Carleton, for helping with last-minute details.

Ruth Carleton

Preface

To K-1-2 teachers and to early readers and their parents:

When I was a mostly first grade teacher for over thirty years in the Palo Alto Unified School District, I wrote twenty-two consecutive little books about the adventures of Penny and Molly — my two dogs who accompanied me to school daily. I often heard students and teachers say how much they would like them in a chapter book. Here it is!

Ruth Carleton

Book 1

Penny and Molly

Hi! I am Penny.
I am a dog.
I like to be a dog.
It is fun.

I have a sister.
Her name is Molly.
Molly is little.
I am big.

We like to play.
We like to play a lot.
We pretend to fight.
We go "Gr-gr-gr-gr!"

I like to go for walks.
I go to Palo Verde School.
It is fun.

At school I see many children.
I like all the children.
They like me too.
We go for walks.

Molly and I have adventures.
You will see all about our adventures.
It will be fun.

Book 2

Penny and Molly Find a Box

Molly said, "Come here, Penny.
I want to play.
I want to play with you."

Penny said, "Let's go!
We can go to the park.
We can play in the park.
We can run and jump.
We can pretend to fight!"

Molly said, "Look, Penny!
I see a box.
I see a big box.
It has a door!"

"Open the door," said
Penny.
"Molly, open the door!
Let's go in the box!"

Molly said, "See the button, Penny.
There is a button.
Push the button, Penny!"
"I'll push it," said Penny.

Wh-r-r-r-r-r-r-r!
Buz-z-z-z-z-z-z-z
Up-up went the box!
Up-up went Penny and Molly!
Where were they going?

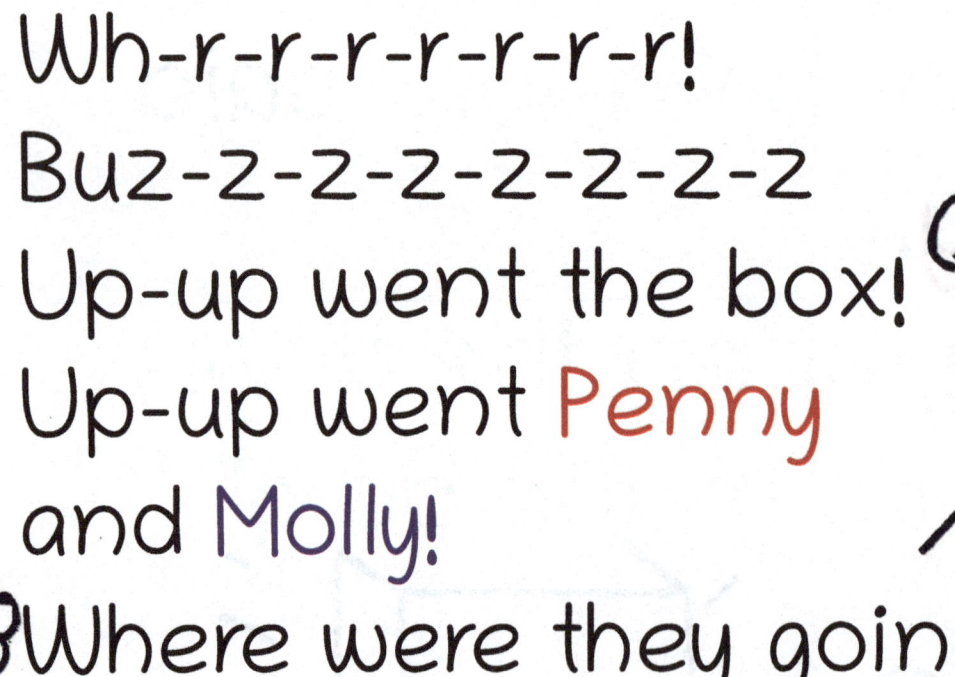

Book 3

Penny and Molly Meet a Friend

The box went up and up.
Penny and Molly were scared!
M-m-m-m-m-m-m.
The box went down.

Penny said, "We can get out."
Molly said, "We can get out of the box."
They got out.

They saw a dinosaur.
It was a big dinosaur.
Molly said, "Let's go!"
Penny said, "Let's go!"

The dinosaur said, "Hi!
I am a good dinosaur.
Come here and see me.
I am a plant eater."

Yum! Yum!

Molly and Penny said,
"Hi! Do you want to play with us?"
"Yes, yes," said the dinosaur.
"I do want to play!"

Molly and Penny and the dinosaur ran.
They jumped.
They played "pretend fight."
Suddenly - - - - - - -
"R-R-R-R-R-Roar!"

Book 4

Penny and Molly Meet T.R.

"R-r-r-r-r-Roar!"
Penny and Molly and the good dinosaur looked up.
What did they see?
Tyrannosaurus Rex!

They were scared!
They ran.
Tyrannosaurus Rex ran.
They came to a big pond.
Dinosaur jumped into it!

"Run to the box, Molly.
Run to the box fast,
Penny!" said Dinosaur.
"Go home, my friends.
Go home!"

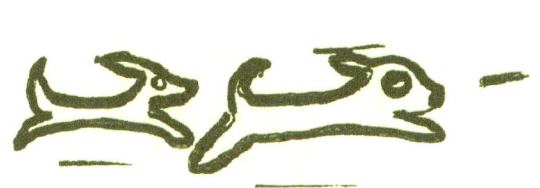

Molly ran fast, fast, fast!
Penny ran fast, fast, fast!
The box was far away.
What could they do?
"R-r-r-r-r-r-Roar!" said T.R.

They got to the box.
They went to the door!
The door would not open.
"Help, help," said Molly.
"Help, help," said Penny.

"Let's pretend to fight," said Molly.
"Gr-r-gr-r-r-r! Gr-r-r-r-r-r!"
They pretended to fight.
T.R. ran away. T.R. was scared.
Penny and Molly got in the box.

Book 5

Penny and Molly Take Off

Penny and Molly got in the box.
"Push the button, Penny," said Molly.
"I'll push it," said Penny.
"Wh-r-r-r-r-r!"
"Buz-z-z-z-z-z!"
Up went the box!

Penny said, "I am glad we got away, Molly.
I am glad we got away from T.R.
   He was big
   He was bad."
"Yes!" said Molly. "I did not like T.R.
But I did like the good dinosaur!"

Up, up went the box.
<u>Up</u> - <u>up</u> - <u>up</u> it went!
It went up and away from the .

It we<u>nt</u> into space!

"Where are we going?" said Penny. "I want to go home!"
"We are going up into space," said Molly. "I think we are going far, far away.
I want to go home, too!"

"M-m-m-m-m-m-m."
The box went down.
Penny and Molly saw some space suits.
Penny and Molly put on the space suits.
"Let's go out," said Molly.

They went out.
They were on the moon.

They saw the U.S. flag.
They saw foot prints.
They saw the 🌍 shining in space.

Book 6

Penny and Molly on the Moon

Penny and Molly looked around.
They saw craters.
They saw mountains.
They saw dust.
There was no air on the moon.

Penny and Molly did not walk.
They bounced.
It was fun to bounce.
"I like it here," said Molly.
"I like it here, too," said Penny.
They pretended to fight.

Suddenly a little man came up!
 "Boo!" he said.
Penny and Molly jumped.
 They were scared!

"I am the man in the moon,"
 said the little man.
 "I am lonely!"
 "Will you play with me?"
 "Yes, yes," said Molly and
 Penny.

Penny and Molly played with the man in the moon.

They played "follow the leader."
They played "hide and go seek."
They had a lot of fun.

Then Penny said, "I want to go home."
Molly said, "O.K., Penny."
"Good-bye, Man in the Moon.
We like you. We want to come back again!"
    They got into the box.

Book 7

Penny and Molly Go to Mars

In the box. Molly said, "Look, Penny! There is a button with 'Mars' on it. Let's go to Mars <u>before</u> we go home."

"O.K.," said Penny. "Let's go to Mars."

So Penny pushed the button.

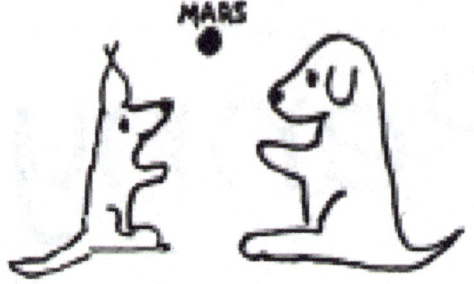

Wh-r-r-r-r-r.

Buzz-z-z-z-z-z.

The box went faster and faster and faster.

Then it went down, down, down.

    Bump! It landed on Mars.

Penny and Molly put on the space suits. They got out of the box. They looked around. They saw red dust. They saw red rocks.

They saw big mountains.

Penny and Molly bounced. They bounced up and down. Molly said, "I can jump like a yo-yo."
She did. She jumped like a yo-yo.

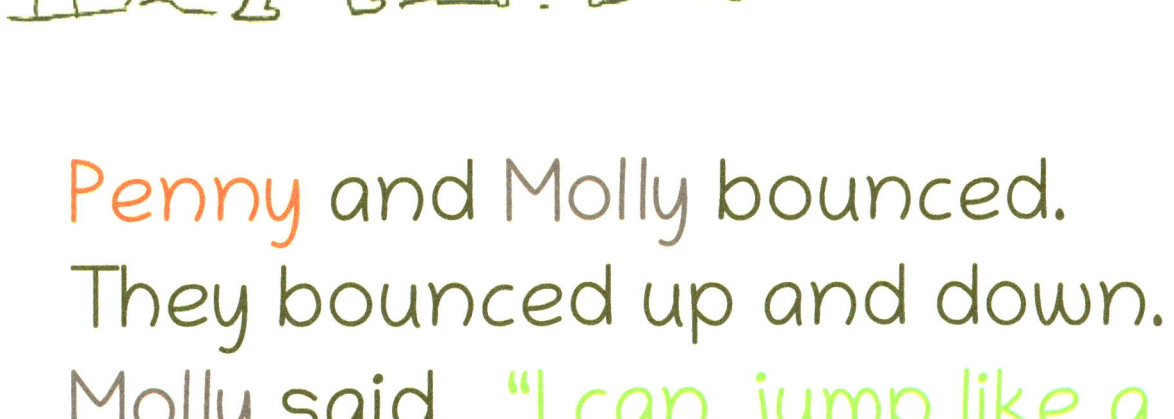

Molly bounced so high.
 Penny could not see her!
"Molly, Molly! Where are you?"
 cried Penny.
Molly had bounced into the crater of an old volcano.

"Oh---oh!" cried Molly. "I am stuck. I can not get out! Help, Penny, help!"
Penny said, "What can I do? I do not have any rope!"
Just then a little voice said,
 "I will help you!"

Book 8

Help from a Martian

Penny looked back. There was a funny little Martian.
She was little. She was red and round.
She hopped on a spring.

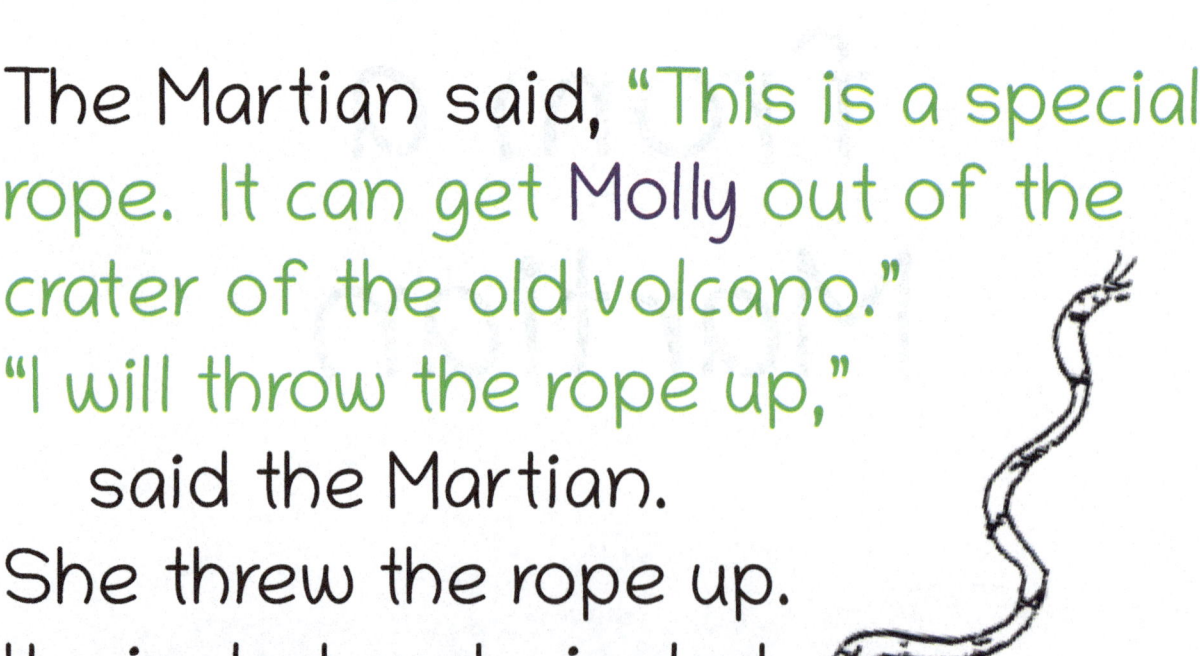

The Martian said, "This is a special rope. It can get Molly out of the crater of the old volcano."
"I will throw the rope up," said the Martian.
She threw the rope up.
It wiggled and wiggled like a snake.

The rope found Molly.
It went around her space suit.
It tugged and tugged.
It tugged Molly out of the crater
Molly bounced back to the
ground.

Penny said, "Wow! That is a good rope. I am glad to see you, Molly! Look, this is the Martian who helped you!"
Molly said, "Oh thank you! thank you."

Penny said to the Martian, "What is your name?"
The Martian said, "My name is Marsy. My pet rope's name is Ropesy. We were happy to help you."

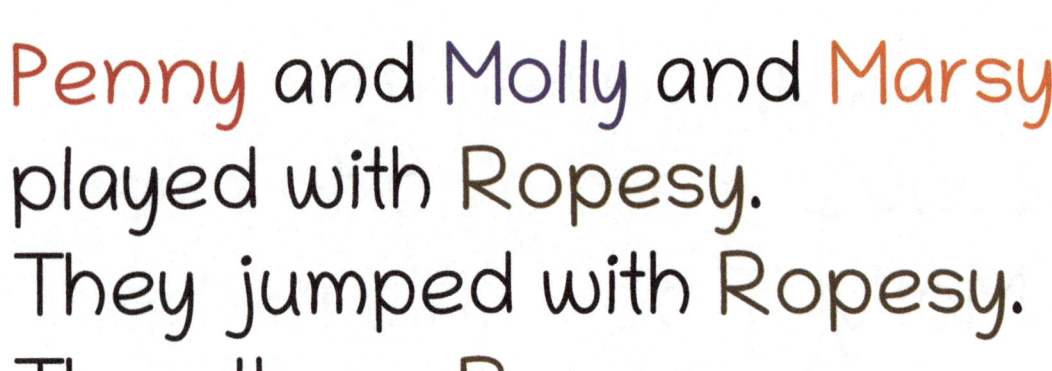

Penny and Molly and Marsy played with Ropesy.
They jumped with Ropesy.
They threw Ropesy up.
They had fun with Ropesy.

Book 9

How About Saturn?

Penny, Molly, Marsy and Ropesy played for a long time.
Then Molly said, "I think it is time for us to go!"
"Oh, no," said Marsy.
"I like you! Please don't go!"

Marsy said, "I have a friend who lives on Saturn. Would you like to go to Saturn with me?"
"Oh, yes, yes!" said Molly and Penny.

Penny, Molly, Marsy and Ropesy
got into the box.
Molly saw a button.
It said "Saturn."
Penny pushed the button.
Up, up, up went the box.
It went up to Saturn.
It took a long time!

The box landed on a
ring of Saturn.
The ring was made of ice.
The friends got out of the box.
Marsy said, "My friend lives
over there on that ring."

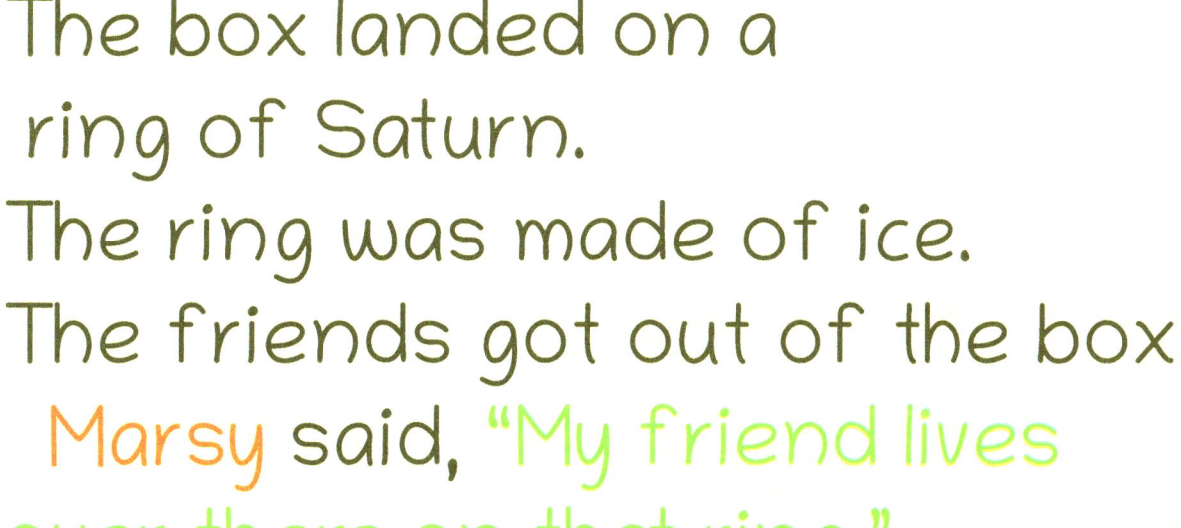

Soon Marsy's friend came over.
He was little and green.
He looked like a triangle.
Marsy said, "This is my friend.
His name is Ringo."
Ringo had 3 feet with
ice skates on them.

Ringo had a bag in his hand.
He said, "Hi! I have some
ice skates for you. We can
skate on Saturn's rings."
Penny, Molly, Marsy and Ringo
held on to Ropesy. They skated
around Saturn's rings!

# Book 10

A Gift from Marsy

Penny, Molly, Marsy and Ropesy had a wonderful time ice skating. They skated around three rings of Saturn. Then Penny said, "This was fun, but it is time for us to go home! Mrs. Carleton and Joe must be missing us."

"I will stay here on Saturn with Ringo," said Marsy. "But you may take my pet rope back to Earth. Maybe Ropesy can help you sometime if you are in danger! Maybe I will come to Earth to visit you."

"Oh, thank you, Marsy," cried Molly and Penny. "We will take good care of Ropesy. And please come visit us on Earth! We would be happy to see you and Ringo too."
Molly and Penny and Ropesy said "Goodbye, Marsy and Ringo!"

They got into the box. Penny pushed a button that said "Earth." Up, up and away went the box. It went faster and faster.
Suddenly something began to pull on the box!
It pulled harder and harder.

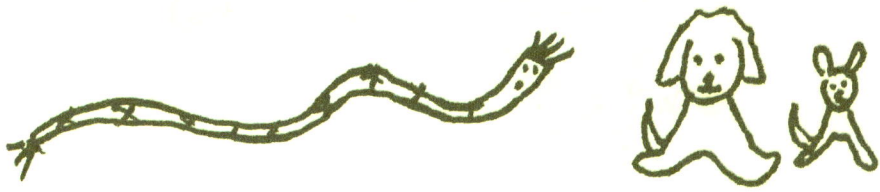

Ropesy cried, "Penny! Molly! We are in the Asteroid Belt. An alien must be trying to get the box! I will go outside and see what it is."

Molly opened the door a little bit.

"Ropesy," said Penny. "I will hold on to the end of you!"

Ropesy slithered out the door. She saw a HUGE alien holding the box! What could Ropesy do?

Book 11

Ropesy Saves the Day

Ropesy was scared, but Ropesy was brave, too.

"What can I do?" asked Ropesy. "I must use my head . . . . . Use my head?? . . . . . That's it," cried Ropesy.

Ropesy had a fuzzy top to her head. She was a frayed rope!

Slowly she slithered up the side of the box.

Slowly she slithered to the HUGE alien's foot, which was holding the box.

She brushed her frayed top on the alien's foot.
The alien began to giggle.
"Tee-hee-hee-hee-hee!"
went the alien.
Ropesy brushed some more!

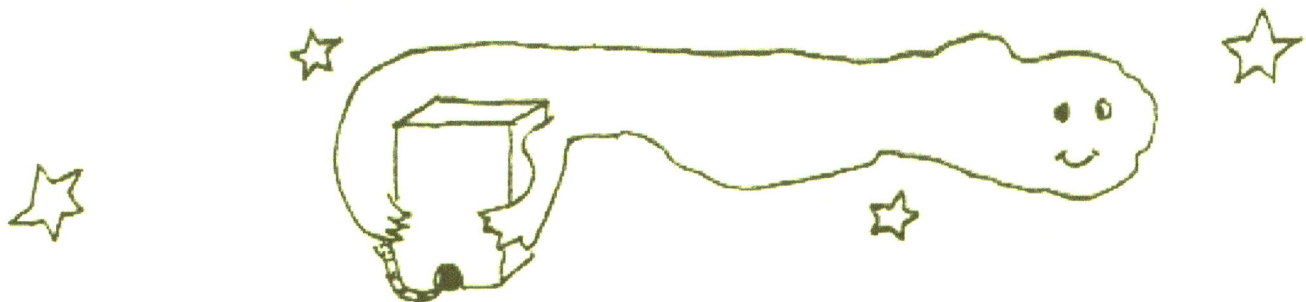

The alien began to laugh hard.
"Ho-ho-ho-hee-hee-ho-ha!"
It could not stand to be tickled any more!
It let go of the box!!

Ropesy went back into the box.
Penny and Molly cheered.
"Hip, hip hoo-ray!
Hip, hip hoo-ray!
Hip, hip hoo-ray! for Ropesy!"
Ropesy was tired, but happy.

Penny pushed a button
that said "Go faster."
The box made a loud roar.
Wh-r-r-r-r-r-r
Buzz-z-z-z-z-z-z
 It zoomed fast.
They were on their way
again.

Book 12

Back to Earth

The box went faster and faster. It was going back to Earth.

"We will be home soon," said Penny.

"I hope so," said Molly.

"I can't wait to see Earth!" said Ropesy.

The box got hot.

"That's because we are in the Earth's atmosphere now," said Molly.

"But don't worry. This is a good box. It has taken us a long way. It will not burn up."

"I wonder if we will land in the park where we found the box," said Penny.

The box was going very fast. Just then it began to go slower.

Suddenly there was a HUGE splash!
Down, down, down went the box! It had not landed in the park. It had landed in the ocean! "Where are we?" asked Penny and Molly.

"Look out the window!"
said Ropesy.
"What window?" asked Penny and Molly.
"That one - - - - behind the panel," said Ropesy.
"We are under water!" they all cried.

Penny and Molly and Ropesy looked out the window.
They saw lots of water.
They saw fish swimming by.
"What can we do?" cried Penny and Molly. "As long as we're here, why don't we explore?" asked Ropesy.

Book 13

An Under-sea Adventure

"Let's explore," cried Ropesy!
"O.K.!" said Molly and Penny.
"But how?"
"Well," replied Ropesy. "You can put on the space suits.
They will work under water, I think."

Penny and Molly put on the space suits.
Ropesy opened the door and slithered out.
Penny and Molly went out quickly and locked the door with a key.
Molly put the key around her neck.

They were on the bottom of the ocean.
The water was a beautiful blue-green color. It was not too cold. It was very beautiful under the ocean.
The friends saw many fish.
They saw many invertebrates.
They saw seaweed.

"Oh, look, Ropesy and Penny!" cried Molly. "Over there! It looks like a beautiful garden."
The garden had a cave by it.
There were rocks with
sea anemones — purple, pink, red, green. They looked like flowers.

There were sea stars on rocks:
orange, red and purple ones.
Penny, Molly and Ropesy stared at the garden.
Just then a deep voice came out of the cave!
"WHAT ARE YOU DOING IN MY GARDEN?"

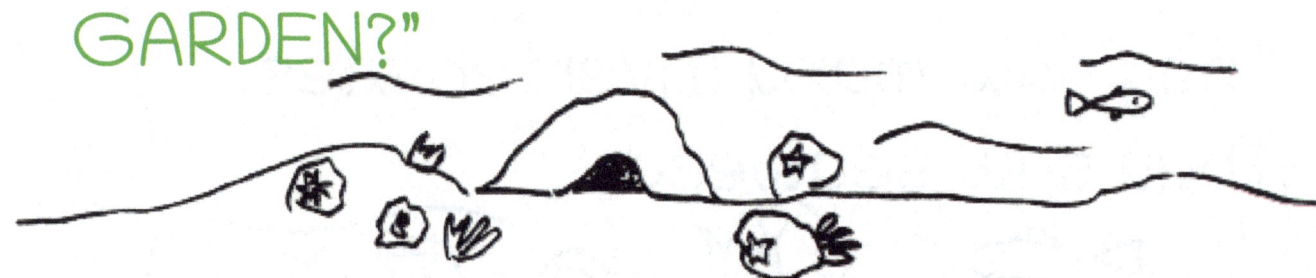

Molly and Penny and Ropesy jumped in alarm!
They stood still.
A long purple thing slithered out of
the cave, and another,
and another, and another,
and another, and another . . .
and another . . . and another.
It was an octopus!

Book 14

A Surprise Friend

"WHAT ARE YOU DOING IN MY GARDEN?" the octopus asked again.
"We are just visiting," replied Molly.
"We are looking at your beautiful garden."
"Ha-rumph!" said the octopus.

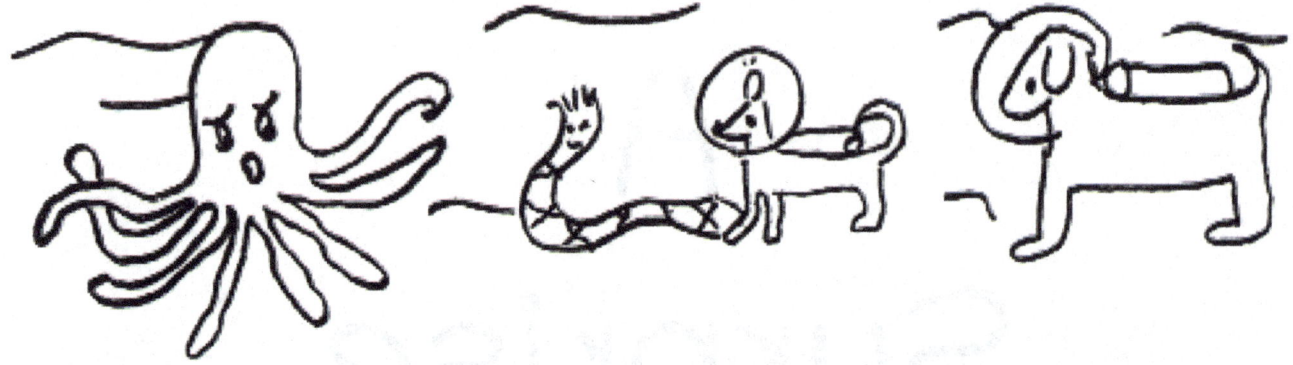

"You are a funny looking fish," the octopus said to Penny and Molly.
"And you are an awfully skinny eel," she said to Ropesy.
"Oh," cried Penny and Molly. "We are not fish. We are dogs — and this is our friend Ropesy."

The octopus began to smile.
"I have heard of dogs before. Are you going to bite me?"
 "Oh, no!" cried Penny and Molly. "We just <u>pretend</u> to bite each other when we pretend to fight."

"Well, then", said the octopus. "We can be friends!"
"Let me show you around."
The octopus showed them his special rocks and sea stars and sea anemones. Then he gave them some seaweed sandwiches and tea. It was yummy!

Then the octopus said, "Would you like to see a ship wreck and a treasure chest? We must be very careful if we do!"

"Yes, yes," cried Penny and Molly and Ropesy.

The octopus and the three friends swam out of the garden. They swam a long way. They saw many interesting things.

They saw jellyfish, squids and many, many fish. Suddenly they saw the wreck!

Book 15

Danger at the Ship Wreck

The octopus, Penny and Molly and Ropesy saw the ship wreck.
It was very, very old. The ship was on its side.
"Come over here," said the octopus. The treasure is on the other side.

The friends swam to the other side of the ship. There was a treasure chest!
Penny and Molly said, "Octopus, can we open the treasure chest and look in?"
"Of course," said the octopus. "I'll help you with my strong arms. I have always wanted to look inside."

They tugged and tugged at the lid of the treasure chest. Suddenly it popped open.

"Oh," cried the friends. "Look at the gold coins! Look at the jewels! There are diamonds and rubies and emeralds!"

Suddenly a huge shadow appeared over the ship wreck. It was a great white shark!

The friends swam into the windows of the wreck.

But the shark could smell that they were there - - - - - -
and the shark was hungry!

"What can we do?" asked Penny, Molly and Ropesy.
"I want to go home," said Penny.
"I will squirt out my ink," said the octopus. "Then we must swim very fast back to my cave. Ropesy must tie us all together or you will get lost."

Ropesy tied the friends together.
The octopus squirted out a lot of black ink.
The great white shark was confused.
It could not find its prey.
All the friends swam to the cave.
They were safe.

60

Book 16

More Trouble!

After the friends got back to the cave, they all rested.

Then Octopus said, "Would you like more tea and seaweed sandwiches?"

"Oh, yes," replied Penny and Molly and Ropesy. "That was quite an adventure!"

After they ate, Molly said,

"Thank you for an exciting time. I think we'd better go back to our box."

"I enjoyed your visit. Please come and see me again," said Octopus.

Molly, Penny and Ropesy said "Good-bye" to Octopus.
They they swam back to the box.
But - - - - - - Molly could not find the key that had been around her neck!

"What can we do? What can we do?" cried Penny and Molly.
"Where did you last see the key, Molly?" asked Ropesy.
"It was at the treasure chest. It must have fallen off when we saw the shark!"

"I will go back," said Ropesy. "The shark will not smell me because I am not an animal. I am a rope. I will go and find the key!"

"You are very brave, Ropesy," cried Penny and Molly.

"We will wait here."

Ropesy swam away to the ship wreck. She was afraid but she was brave. She went to the other side of the ship wreck, but she could not find the key. She was about to give up when she heard a great ROAR!

Book 17

Ropesy Saves the Day Again

"Ow-w-ow-ow!" It was the shark! Ropesy hid by a rock.

"Ow-ow-ow-w-w!" went the shark. Ropesy looked at the shark.

"I think that shark has a tummy ache!" Ropesy said to herself.

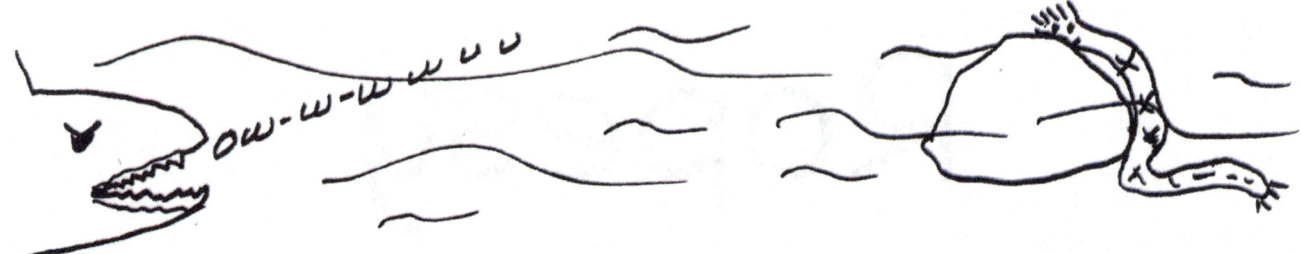

Ropesy slithered up to the shark. It did not see her. The shark opened its mouth wide.

"Ow-ow-w-w-w-w-w-w!" Ropesy went into the shark's mouth. She tickled the shark's throat.

The shark began to cough and sneeze. "Ah ——— chooooooo!"

Out came Ropesy.

Out came the key.

The shark swam away, happy. Ropesy grabbed the key and swam back to the box.

Penny and Molly saw Ropesy coming.

They saw the key around her neck.

"Oh, Ropesy, you found the key. You are back safe. We were so worried!"

Hip-hip hooray for Ropesy!
Hip-hip hooray!
Hip-hip hooray!

"What happened? How did you find it?" asked the friends.

"It's a long story," said Ropesy. "Let's get into the box first."

So they did. Then Ropesy told them all about the great white shark and its tummy ache.

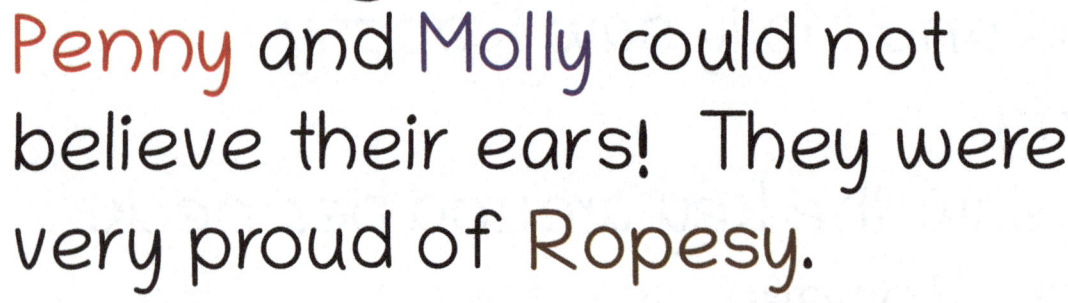

Penny and Molly could not believe their ears! They were very proud of Ropesy.

"Let's go home," said Penny.
So she pushed a button.
    Glug-glug-
    Wh-r-r-r-r-r
    They were off!

Book 18

Can It Be True?

Up-up-up went the box.
through the blue-green water
of the ocean.

Splash! Out of the water it rose
into the sky.
Penny, Molly and Ropesy were tired.
They fell asleep.

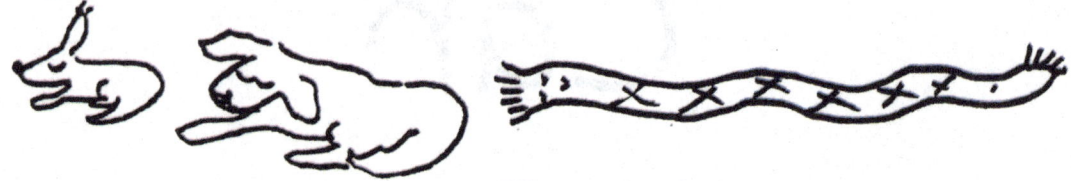

Penny woke up suddenly. The
box was not moving. There was
not a sound. Penny woke up
Molly and Ropesy.

"Where are we?" they cried.
They were almost afraid to look
outside.

Finally Ropesy said, "It's now or never! I want to see what Earth looks like. Let's go!"

So Penny and Molly and Ropesy opened the door.

What do you think they saw?

They were in the park!

"We're home!" they shouted.

"We're home at last!"

Ropesy could not believe her eyes.

"What is that funny green stuff on the ground?" she asked.

"That is grass," replied Penny and Molly.

Ropesy slithered along the grass. "It tickles," she said.

Suddenly along came a gardener.
 He was cutting the grass. He saw Ropesy slithering through the grass. He thought she was a snake — a dangerous snake!

Penny and Molly saw the gardener. They saw that Ropesy was in great danger.

 "What can we do?" they asked.

Penny and Molly began to bark!
 The gardener looked up just as he was about to cut Ropesy to pieces.

Ropesy went away as fast as she could go. She slid down a hole. But - - - - - MORE DANGER!!!

Book 19

Down the Hole

Ropesy slid down a long, dark tunnel. It was so smooth it was like a sliding board.
"Where on Earth am I going?" thought Ropesy. "The end must come sooner or later!"

Finally Ropesy came to the bottom. She was in a cave! It was lit with a strange green light.
"I think I will wait here before I try to get out."
Ropesy felt tired. She coiled herself up for a quick nap.
"Maybe I will think of something to do if I rest," she said.

Meanwhile, up in the park, Penny and Molly waited for the gardener to go away. When he left for another part of the park, Molly and Penny went to the hole. They looked in, but it was very dark and they could not see Ropesy at all!

Molly said, "I think we better start to dig."
So they began to dig. They dug and dug for a long time.
At last they had made the hole big enough to go in. They began to slide down the tunnel. It was scary but fun too.

Bump! They landed at the bottom of the tunnel. They were in a big cave.
"Look! Over there! It's Ropesy!"
They ran over to Ropesy who was sound asleep.
"Ropesy, Ropesy, It's us," they cried. "We have come to help you out."

"Thank goodness you're here!" said Ropesy. "But now we have to get all three of us out."
"It should be easy," said Molly. "We can just crawl up the tunnel."
"But it is very steep and slippery," replied Ropesy.
Just then a voice said, "You are not going anywhere!"

Book 20

What
Is
It?

"YOU ARE NOT GOING ANYWHERE!" the voice repeated.

Penny, Molly and Ropesy turned around slowly.

There was a very prickly, very cross-looking thing!

"Wh-wh-wh-wh-who are you?" they stammered.

"I am Go-Lo. I am the King of the underground. Once someone comes into my cave, they can never go back to their home again. I will put you into a little cave. You must stay there until I call for you!"

King Go-Lo led the three friends into a little cave with bars.
He locked the door and was quickly gone.
The three friends looked at each other.
"We are in quite a predicament," said Molly.
"I want to go home," said Penny.

Ropesy said, "We must all use our heads to figure out how to get out of this mess!"
The three friends rested for a while. Then they heard footsteps. It was a little prickly thing. It said, "Come with me. King Go-Lo wishes to see you."

They found King Go-Lo sitting on a rock throne. There were many little go-los around the throne.
They were all cross-looking.
King Go-Lo said, "Since you are here, I want you to entertain us. But you cannot make us laugh, because no go-lo has ever laughed before."

Ropesy whispered to Penny and Molly, "I have an idea. Maybe if we can make the Go-Los laugh, we will be allowed to leave, or at least we can escape!"
"But how on Earth can we make them laugh? We are just dogs and a rope. What's funny about that?"

Book 21

Will They Laugh?

King Go-Lo shouted in a loud voice, "Begin to entertain us!" Ropesy whispered to Penny and Molly, "These poor Go-Los never have any fun. That's why they don't laugh. Let's play jump-rope with them!" Penny took one end of Ropesy. Molly took the other end. They got one little Go-Lo to jump. It was hard, at first. Then he caught on.

The Go-Los got in a line to take turns. They jumped many times. They did not look quite as cross. Then King Go-Lo said, "I want to try that too!" He did <u>and</u> he was a very good jumper. He even did a little twist in the middle of his jump!

Then Ropesy said, "Everyone grab hold of me, Penny first." Penny ran very fast. Molly did too. All the Go-Los hung on to Ropesy or each other.
Faster, faster they ran! The Go-Los on the end could not stay on the ground. They shrieked with excitement!

At last they all fell down in a heap. Ropesy began to tickle the Go-Los with her frayed ends. One little Go-Lo began to giggle softly, "Tee-hee-hee-hee." Another Go-Lo giggled a little louder. A third Go-Lo giggled very loudly! Soon the heap was a mass of giggles. The King was the loudest of all!

At last King Go-Lo shouted with a loud laugh, "We must be laughing! Is this what laughing is? It feels good! It's fun! It makes me - - - - HAPPY! But - but - that means we will have to let you go!! And you are the ones who made us laugh. Now we will never laugh again!"

"No, no!" said Molly and Penny and Ropesy. "You can have fun yourselves! Look, you can climb up and down stalagmites and stalactites. You can slide down the tunnel. You can play Follow the leader and Hide and go-seek!"

"But what about jump-rope? We have no jump rope. What can we do????"

Book 22

What Next?

"I have an idea," said Molly. "King Go-Lo, when we go home, we will ask Joe and Mrs. Carleton for some rope. Joe has a lot of rope around the house."

"Yes," said Penny. "I used to chew it when I was a puppy. I'm sorry, Ropesy — hope you don't mind!"

"Not at all," replied Ropesy. "I think that's just the way puppies are!"

"Anyhow, King Go-Lo, we will put a nice, big rope down the hole. Then you will have a rope to play with!"

"Is that a promise?" asked King Go-Lo.

"Of course," the friends replied.

"I have another idea," said Ropesy.

"Can you Go-Los read?"

"Naturally," answered the King.

"Then we will get Mrs. Carleton to write funny jokes for you from time to time. If she will, that is! We will throw them down the hole," said Ropesy.
"Hmmmm, that sounds great," said the King. "It's a deal."
"Now we will help you go up the tunnel because it is steep and slippery."

So they all said "Good-bye." The Go-Los looked happy. Some of the Go-Los hung on to the tunnel with their sharp claws so the friends could climb up on them. Slowly they made their way up the tunnel. At last they were back in the park. It was almost dark.

Penny and Molly led Ropesy to their house. The light was on. They scratched on the door. Joe came to answer.
"Ruth, look here!
It's our dogs. They have come home at last. Where were you, Penny and Molly, and what is this - - - - - - - a rope???"

Joe and Mrs. Carleton were full of questions.
Penny and Molly and Ropesy were full of answers.
But they had a few questions of their own.
Such as . . . would they ever see the Moon Man, Marsy, Ringo, Octopus and the Go-Los again?
And what would their next adventures be?

Teacher's Guide

Note: These are brief notes for teachers and parents with ideas for lesson plans and key ideas for each of the Penny and Molly stories.

Book 1: Penny and Molly

A dog has a backbone. So it is a <u>vertebrate</u>. A dog is a <u>mammal</u>.

Mammals:
1. Breathe oxygen from air.
2. Have fur or hair.
3. Have babies born alive.
4. Have mothers that make milk.

As a human being, you are a mammal too.

Book 2: Penny and Molly Find a Box

Caretakers should warn children never to get in a box because of the danger of suffocation.

Book 3: Penny and Molly Meet a Friend

Dinosaurs do not live anymore.
They are <u>extinct</u>.
Some dinosaurs are plant eaters.
A plant eater is a <u>herbivore</u>.

Book 4: Penny and Molly Meet T.R.

A meat-eating dinosaur is a <u>carnivore</u>.
A <u>Tyrannosaurus rex</u> is a carnivore.
An animal that eats plants and animals is an <u>omnivore</u>.

Book 5: Penny and Molly Take Off

A spaceship must go beyond the earth's gravity to get to the moon.

Gravity is the force that holds us on planet Earth.

The first astronauts to land on the moon left their footprints on the moon because there is no air there, and hence no wind to blow the footprints away.

Book 6: Penny and Molly on the Moon

The moon is a satellite, which means it goes around the Earth. That's why the moon looks different during the course of the month.

There is less gravity on the moon, so you bounce when you walk on it.

Book 7: Penny and Molly Go to Mars

Take a look at a diagram of the <u>solar system</u>. Locate Mars.

Mars has less gravity force (like the moon), so you would bounce when you walk there.

A <u>volcano</u> is a mountain that connects inside the earth.

This is an extinct volcano.

Book 8: Help from a Martian

There are really — as far as we know — no living creatures on Mars, but scientists keep hoping to find life there.

Book 9: How About Saturn?

Saturn is far away.

Its rings may be made of ice.

Book 10: A Gift from Marsy

An <u>alien</u> is a stranger.
The <u>asteroid belt</u> is a part of space where there are many asteroids (parts of planets).

Book 11: Ropesy Saves the Day

Look at a rope. See if it has a fuzzy end. If it does, it is <u>frayed</u>.

Demonstrate the word <u>slither</u>.

Book 12: Back to Earth

Why do you think some spaceships land in the ocean?

The <u>atmosphere</u> is like an envelope around the Earth.

Why does a spaceship get hot going through the atmosphere?

Book 13: An Under-sea Adventure

An <u>Invertebrate</u> has no back bone.

Here are some Invertebrates in the ocean.

> Octopus
> Squid
> Crabs
> Sea Stars
> Sea Anemones

Book 14: A Surprise Friend

Some facts about an octopus:
> 1. It does not have a backbone.
> 2. It has eight arms (<u>octo</u> means eight).
> 3. The arms have suction cups on them.

4. An octopus can squirt out an inklike substance to confuse enemies.
5. It is one of the most intelligent invertebrates.
6. It can squeeze its body into small spaces.

Book 15: Danger at the Ship Wreck

A shark is a predator.
An octopus could be its prey.

An octopus can be a predator to small creatures.

Book 16: More Trouble!

How does <u>memory</u> help?

When you lose something, it helps to think where you last saw the object.

Book 17: Ropesy Saves the Day Again

What can make you cough or sneeze?
How does a cough or sneeze help you?

Book 18: Can It Be True?

Grass is an amazing plant in these ways:
    1. It is beautiful.
    2. It can be food for animals.
    3. It breathes in carbon dioxide and exhales oxygen, which all animals need to live.
    4. It absorbs water, which might otherwise sometimes cause floods.
    5. It is nice to play on.

Book 19: Down the Hole

The Earth is not a solid ball. It has different layers. Sometimes it has caves in it made by water.

Book 20: What Is It?

Problem solving is an important skill:

    1. Identify the problem.
    2. Think of two or three possible solutions.
    3. Choose one solution. If it doesn't work, try another.

Book 21: Will They Laugh?

Why does laughing make us feel good?
Stalactite: V

Stalagmite: Λ

Book 22: What Next?

What adventures will come next?
How do we make plans for the future?

Made in the USA
Coppell, TX
20 February 2026